Mario Botta

Mario Botta

teNeues

Editor in chief:
Paco Asensio

Editor and original texts:
Aurora Cuito

English translation:
William Bain

German translation:
Martin Fischer

French translation:
Agencia Lingo Sense

Italian translation:
Grazia Sufritti

Art direction:
Mireia Casanovas Soley

Graphic Design / Layout:
Emma Termes Parera and Soti Mas-Bagà

Published worldwide by teNeues Publishing Group
(except Spain, Portugal and South-America):

teNeues Book Division
Kaistraße 18, 40221 Düsseldorf, Germany
Tel.: 0049-(0)211-994597-0
Fax: 0049-(0)211-994597-40

teNeues Publishing Company
16 West 22nd Street, New York, N.Y., 10010, USA
Tel.: 001-212-627-9090
Fax: 001-212-627-9511

teNeues Publishing UK Ltd.
P.O. Box 402
West Byfleet
KT14 7ZF
Tel.: 0044-1932-403509
Fax: 0044-1932-403514

teNeues France S.A.R.L.
140, rue de la Croix Nivert
75015 Paris, France
Tel.: 0033-1-5576-6205
Fax: 0033-1-5576-6419

www.teneues.com

Editorial project:

© 2003 **LOFT** Publications
Via Laietana, 32 4° Of. 92
08003 Barcelona, Spain
Tel.: 0034 932 688 088
Fax: 0034 932 687 073
e-mail: loft@loftpublications.com
www.loftpublications.com

Printed by:
Anman Gràfiques del Vallès, Spain
June 2003

Bibliographic information published by Die Deutsche Bibliothek
Die Deutsche Bibliothek lists this publication in the Deutsche
Nationalbibliografie; detailed bibliographic data is available in the
Internet at http://dnb.ddb.de.

ISBN: 3-8238-4537-3

We would like to show sincere gratefulness to the office of Mario
Botta, specially to Paola Pellandini for her useful collaboration.

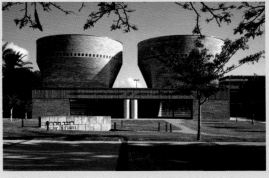

At an early age, Mario Botta already showed a special interest for architecture and the arts. This may be seen in his first work as a technical draftsman and his studies at the Liceo Artistico in Milan. His youthful apprenticeship came to an end when he received his degree in architecture at the University of Venice and began his collaborations in the offices of Le Corbusier and Louis Kahn. The choice of these two studios is hardly casual: at this early stage, Botta had decided to learn from two of the great masters of modern architecture. Their teachings would become reference points in his professional career.

This influence by rationalism, however, will not cause the Swiss architect to forget his sensitivity for place, topographical conditions, and native building techniques. These features make up a basic part of his vision and are largely what fuse modernity and tradition in his work.

All of Mario Botta's projects, from the design of clocks, passing through the small one-family homes in the Alpine region of Ticino, and on to the large museums such as the San Francisco MOMA, are subtended by one and the same determination: reconciling geometry, order, and function with imagination, symbolism, and poetry.

Mario Botta zeigte schon sehr früh Interesse für Kunst und Architektur. Er arbeitete zunächst als technischer Zeichner und besuchte die Kunstschule in Mailand. Anschließend studierte er Architektur an der Universität Venedig und arbeitete in den Büros von Le Corbusier und Louis Kahn. Die Wahl dieser beiden Büros geschah keinesfalls zufällig, denn der junge Botta nahm sich vor, von den großen Meistern der modernen Architektur zu lernen. Ihre Lehren wurden zum Bezugspunkt für seine spätere berufliche Laufbahn.

Der Einfluss des Rationalismus hat ihn allerdings nicht unempfindlich gemacht gegenüber dem Geist des Ortes, den topographischen Gegebenheiten und den überlieferten einheimischen Bauformen. In seinen Bauten fließen Moderne und Tradition zusammen.

Alle Entwürfe Bottas – vom Uhrdesign über kleine Einfamilienhäuser im Tessin bis hin zu den großen Museen wie dem MOMA von San Francisco – verbindet dasselbe Grundprinzip: die Suche nach der Aussöhnung von Geometrie, Ordnung und Funktionalität mit Fantasie, Symbolik und Poesie.

Très jeune, Mario Botta a fait montre d'un intérêt spécial pour l'architecture et les arts. Comme il le prouve dans son premier travail de dessinateur technique et ses études au Lycée artistique de Milan. Son apprentissage culmine avec une maîtrise en architecture de l'Université de Venise et des collaborations dans les études de Le Corbusier et Louis Kahn. Le choix de ces deux ateliers n'est pas neutre. En effet, le jeune Botta décide d'apprendre des deux grands maîtres de l'architecture moderne, dont les enseignements vont se convertir en des référents tout au long de sa carrière professionnelle.

L'influence du rationalisme ne l'a pourtant pas fait renoncer à la sensibilité envers le lieu, les conditions topographiques et les techniques de construction autochtones afin de créer des œuvres conjuguant modernité et tradition.

Tous les projets de Mario Botta, du design de montres jusqu'aux grands musées comme le MOMA de San Francisco, en passant par les petites maisons particulières de la région alpine de Tessin, sont régis par une même détermination : réconcilier la géométrie, l'ordre et la fonctionnalité avec l'imagination, le symbolisme et la poésie.

Fin da molto giovane Mario Botta ha mostrato uno speciale interesse per l'architettura e l'arte, come dimostrano il suo primo lavoro come disegnatore tecnico, ed i suoi studi al Liceo artistico di Milano. Il suo apprendistato giovanile ha raggiunto l'apice con la laurea in architettura nell'Università di Venezia e con la collaborazione negli studi di Le Corbusier e Louis Kahn. La scelta di questi due laboratori non è casuale: il giovane Botta decide di imparare da due dei grandi maestri dell'architettura moderna, i cui insegnamenti si sono trasformati in un punto di riferimento durante tutta la sua traiettoria professionale.

Ciò nonostante, l'influenza del razionalismo non gli ha fatto rinunciare alla sensibilità per il territorio, per le condizioni topografiche e per le tecniche costruttive autoctone, riuscendo così a modellare opere che coniugano modernità e tradizione.

Tutti i progetti di Mario Botta, dal design di orologi, passando attraverso le piccole case unifamiliari nella regione alpina del Ticino, fino ai grandi musei come il MOMA di San Francisco, sono retti da una stessa determinazione: riconciliare la geometria, l'ordine e la funzionalità con l'immaginazione, il simbolismo e la poesia.

San Francisco Museum of Modern Art

Location: 151 Third Street, San Francisco, California, USA
Date of construction: 1992–1995
Photographers: Pino Musi, Robert Canfield

Dropping the museum into a space already containing three very tall buildings led to the design of a project that is formally peculiar. It stands out because of the power of the image yet defies comparison with its immediate environment. Point zero found the architect and the clients setting three clear aims: natural lighting, in the first place, must predominate in spite of the unfavorable façade-surface relation. To satisfy this need, the idea came about of a skylight system that would figure in almost every exhibition room. The result would be diffuse natural light, the ideal setting for works of art. Aim two: the façades needed to be homogeneous and still stimulate visitors to go in and walk around the incredible installations. Textured brickwork provided the answer for one part of the edifice; the blending of two types of marble was agreed for the remaining part. This brings about a coherent exterior aesthetic that is both attractive and unique. Final objective: a unifying interior image will be generated to harmonize the different parts of the museum: to carry this out, they restricted the array of materials that go into the final figuration of facings.

Das neue Museum sollte in unmittelbarer Nachbarschaft zu drei Hochhäusern errichtet werden. Bottas Entwurf sah deshalb einen formal ausdrucksstarken Bau vor, der für sich alleine stehen und dem Vergleich mit den angrenzenden Bauten standhalten kann. Architekt und Bauherr legten gleich zu Beginn drei Ziele fest, die die Entwurfsplanung bestimmten: Die Ausstellungsräume brauchten natürliches Licht, die Außenfassade sollte homogen und einladend erscheinen und das Innere des Museums erforderte eine harmonische Gestaltung. Wegen des ungünstigen Verhältnisses von der Fassaden- zur Geschossfläche war der Wunsch nach natürlichem Licht nicht leicht zu erfüllen. Doch der Architekt ersann ein System von Oberlichtern, durch die fast alle Ausstellungsräume mit einem diffusen Licht ausgestattet wurden, wie es für Kunstwerke am besten geeignet ist. Für die Fassadengestaltung griff Botta bei Teilen des Gebäudes auf Backstein und bei anderen auf die Kombination zweier Arten von Marmor zurück. So gelang es ihm, ein in ästhetischer Hinsicht kohärentes und zugleich auffälliges und unverwechselbares Äußeres zu schaffen. Schließlich ging es um die Schaffung eines einheitlichen Erscheinungsbildes aller Innenräume der verschiedenen Abteilungen des Museums. Dies wurde durch eine begrenzte Auswahl miteinander kombinierter Materialien erreicht.

La situation du musée, entre trois bâtiments très élevés, engendra un projet au concept formel particulier, soulignant une image puissante tout en évitant toute comparaison avec son voisinage immédiat. Depuis le départ, architecte et clients ont fixé trois objectifs clairs : en premier lieu, l'illumination naturelle devait dominer en dépit d'une proportion façade/superficie défavorable. Afin de satisfaire à cette obligation, fut conçu un système de claires-voies présent dans presque toutes les salles d'exposition. Il offre une lumière diffuse, optimale pour les œuvres d'art. Les façades devaient, par surcroît, être homogènes en étant capables d'inciter les visiteurs à s'aventurer dans les installations. Botta eut recours à la brique pour une partie du bâtiment et à une combinaison de deux marbres différents pour l'autre. Il obtint ainsi une esthétique extérieure cohérente et à la fois éloquente et caractéristique. Il fallait enfin générer une image intérieure unitaire, afin d'harmoniser les différentes parties du musée. Botta sélectionna donc une palette restreinte de matériaux, associés pour proposer la finition.

La collocazione del museo, fra tre edifici di notevole altezza, ha portato all'elaborazione di un progetto formalmente singolare, che emerge con una potente figura ed allo stesso tempo esclude il confronto con l'ambiente circostante. Fin dal principio architetto e clienti fissarono tre obiettivi chiari: in primo luogo l'illuminazione naturale doveva predominare nonostante la proporzione sfavorevole facciata-superficie. Per soddisfare questo requisito è stato progettato un sistema di lucernari presente in quasi tutte le sale d'esposizione, che fornisce una luce diffusa, ottima per le opere d'arte. Inoltre era richiesto che le facciate fossero omogenee ed allo stesso tempo incoraggiassero i visitatori ad entrare negli allestimenti. Si è utilizzato il mattone per una parte della costruzione e la combinazione di due tipi di marmo nell'altra. In questo modo si è ottenuta un'estetica esterna coerente ed allo stesso tempo appariscente e inconfondibile. Per ultimo si doveva creare un'immagine interna unitaria che legasse le differenti parti del museo, per far ciò è stata selezionata una ristretta gamma di materiali che sono stati abbinati per uniformare le finiture.

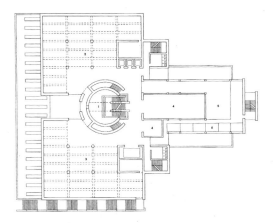

Fourth floor
Viertes Obergeschoss
Quatrième étage
Piano quarto

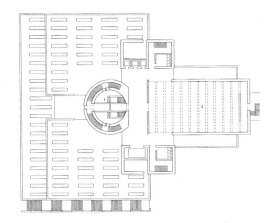

Fifth floor
Fünftes Obergeschoss
Cinquième étage
Piano quinto

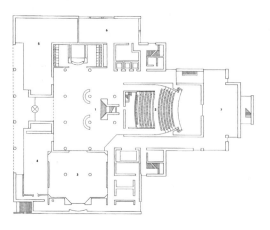

Ground floor
Erdgeschoss
Rez-de-chaussée
Piano terra

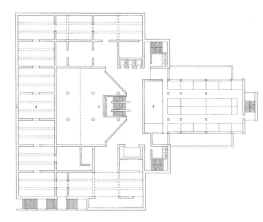

Second floor
Zweites Obergeschoss
Deuxième étage
Piano secondo

0   5   10

Chapel of Saint Mary of the Angels

Location: Alpe Foppa, Monte Tamaro, Ticino, Switzerland
Date of construction: 1992–1996
Photographers: Enrico Cano, Pino Musi

The chapel is located at the exit of the funicular railway linking the mountain localities of Rivera and Alpe Foppa. It is a project that came out of the commission given to Botta by the owner of these installations. Emerging from the mountain through the 65-meter long viaduct, one reaches a lookout point which has a set of steps that lead down the roof to the hermitage. A bell seated in a metallic structure marks the beginning of the stairs and anticipates the chapel's placement, hidden away by the difference in grade. Cylindrical in shape, the chapel, which is 15 meters in diameter, is divided into a tripartite plan. Two of these rooms are perimeter walkways; the other forms the central nave. At one end of the cylinder is a small apse with a skylight that inundate the place with natural light. The artist Enzo Cucchi was commissioned to paint a large mural behind the altar and some panels that were then located on the lateral window aisles. Cucchi was also responsible for the decoration of the vaulted ceiling of the central part and the drawings in the entrance gallery.

Die Kapelle liegt am Ausgang der Bergstation der Drahtseilbahn, die Rivera mit Alpe Foppa verbindet. Sie entstand im Auftrag des Eigentümers der Seilbahn. Über einen 65 m langen aus dem Berg ragenden Viadukt erreicht man eine Aussichtsplattform von der Stufen zur Einsiedelkapelle hinabführen. Oben an der Treppe deutet eine in einer Metallkonstruktion aufgehängte Glocke schon auf die Kapelle hin, die dem Blick durch den Höhenunterschied noch verborgen bleibt. Der Bau besteht aus einem Zylinder von 15 m Durchmesser, der im Inneren in drei Bereiche gegliedert wird: zwei äußere Wandelgänge und das Mittelschiff. Am einen Ende des Zylinders ist eine kleine Apsis angefügt, deren Oberlicht das Innere mit natürlichem Licht erfüllt. Der Künstler Enzo Cucchi schuf ein großformatiges Wandbild hinter dem Altar und Tafeln in den seitlichen Fensternischen. Cucchi war auch verantwortlich für die Ausmalung der gewölbten Decke des Kirchenraums und der Eingangsgalerie.

La chapelle est située à la sortie du funiculaire, unissant les localités alpines de Rivera et de Alpe Foppa. Elle correspond à une commande du propriétaire des installations. Par un viaduc long de 65 mètres, l'on accède à un mirador duquel des marches descendent vers l'entrée de l'hermitage. Une cloche supportée par une structure métallique marque le début de la montée et anticipe sur l'existence de la chapelle, qui demeure cachée par la dénivellation. Le volume de la construction propose un cylindre de 15 mètres de diamètre divisé en trois zones, deux périmètres de circulation et une nef centrale. À la fin du cylindre se trouve une petite abside dont le lanternau l'inondent de lumière naturelle. L'artiste Enzo Cucchi fut chargé de la grande peinture murale derrière l'autel et de panneaux disposés dans les niches des fenêtres laterales. Cucchi est également l'auteur de la peinture du toit voûté de la partie centrale et de la galerie d'entrée.

La cappella è situata all'uscita della funivia che unisce le località alpine di Rivera e Alpe Foppa ed è sorta per incarico del proprietario degli impianti. Un viadotto di 65 metri porta ad un belvedere dal quale si accede alle scale che scendono verso l'eremo. Una campana sostenuta da una struttura metallica marca l'inizio della scalinata e anticipa l'esistenza della cappella, che rimane nascosta dal dislivello. Il volume della costruzione è composto da un cilindro di 15 metri di diametro diviso in tre aree, due perimetrali di circolazione ed una navata centrale. Alla fine del cilindro si trova una piccola abside con un lucernario che la inonda di luce naturale. L'artista Enzo Cucchi è stato incaricato di dipingere un grande affresco dietro all'altare e delle che sono stati collocati nelle nicchie delle finestrelle laterali. Cucchi è anche l'autore dei affreschi del tetto a volta della parte centrale e nella galleria d'entrata.

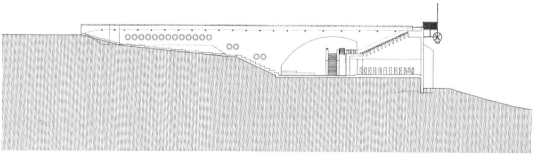

Longitudinal section   Längsschnitt

Section longitudinale   **Sezione longitudinale**

0   5   10

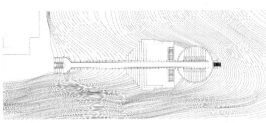

Roof plan
Grundriss and Dacher
Niveau supérieur
Pianta delle coperture

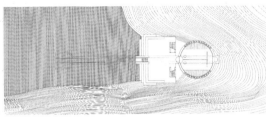

Ground floor
Erdgeschoss
Rez-de-chaussée
Piano terra

0　5　10

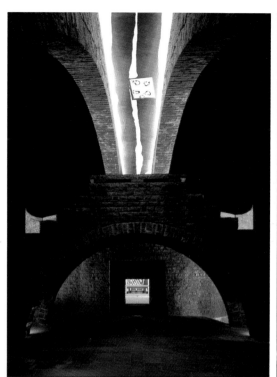

Church of Saint John the Baptist

Location: Mogno-Fusio, Maggia, Ticino, Switzerland
Date of construction: 1992–1998
Photographer: Pino Musi

This small church stands in the upper part of the Maggia Valley, at the foot of the Italian Alps. It replaces the old seventeenth-century church that disappeared, along with part of the village of Mogno, in a devastating avalanche in 1986. The dramatic causes underlying the commission to build a new also led to the need to take special care in relation to the setting of the building, to the building techniques used in the work, and to the expression, both physical and symbolic, of the complex within such a breathtakingly beautiful natural environment. Botta chose to develop a structure using large stone walls, buttressed, and covered with a roof of light glass. It is a contrast that brings out the fragility of humankind before the forces of nature; it also stems, perhaps, from an attempt to bring each individual a place from which to communicate with God as an equal. The ground floor is ordered by simple geometric forms: a rectangle inscribed in an ellipse which, on the roof, becomes a circumference. This compositional clarity sees itself underscored by the simple construction system, which provides the required resistance.

Diese kleine Kirche liegt im oberen Maggia-Tal am Fuße der italienischen Alpen und ersetzt die ehemalige Kirche aus dem 17. Jahrhundert, die 1986 zusammen mit einem Teil des Dorfes Mogno von einer verheerenden Lawine zerstört worden war. Dieser tragische Hintergrund bestimmte in mehrfacher Hinsicht die Entwurfsplanung: Es wurde nicht nur besonderes Augenmerk auf die bautechnischen Einzelheiten gerichtet, sondern auch auf den Bezug zur Umgebung. Der Sakralbau sollte sowohl physisch als auch symbolisch eine Einheit mit der atemberaubenden Landschaft bilden. Botta entschied sich für feste Steinmauern mit verstärkenden Strebepfeilern und ein leichtes Glasdach. In diesem Kontrast der Materialien wird die Ohnmacht des Menschen angesichts der Naturgewalten widergespiegelt und zugleich wird ihm ein Ort gegeben, an dem er von Angesicht zu Angesicht mit Gott sprechen kann. Der Grundriss folgt einfachen geometrischen Formen: Ein Rechteck ist in eine Ellipse eingeschrieben, die zum Dach hin zu einem Kreis wird. Die klare Formensprache entspricht damit dem einfachen Bauprinzip, das der erforderlichen Standfestigkeit genügen muss.

Cette petite église est située dans la partie haute de la vallée de Maggia, au pied des Alpes italiennes. Elle se substitue à l'ancienne église du XVIIème siècle disparue avec une partie du village de Mogno dans une avalanche destructrice, en 1986. Les causes dramatiques à l'origine de la commandes ont impliqué une attention particulière à la relation entre l'édifice et son environnement et aux techniques de construction prévue pour les travaux. Elles ont également défini l'expression physique comme symbolique devant être adoptée par l'ensemble dans un cadre naturel si prenant. Botta s'est décidé pour un bâtiment composé de grands murs de pierre, soutenus par des arcs-boutants et d'une légère toiture vitrée. Ce contraste matérialise la fragilité de l'homme face aux forces de la nature. Mais il tend aussi à offrir à l'individu un lieu pour communiquer avec Dieu, d'égal à égal. Le niveau est régi par des formes géométriques simples : un rectangle inscrit dans une ellipse se transforment, pour la toiture, en une circonférence. La clarté de la composition est accentuée par un système architectural simple, offrant la résistance requise.

Questa piccola chiesa è situata nella parte alta della valle di Maggia, ai piedi delle Alpi italiane, e sostituisce l'antica chiesa del XVII° secolo. Che sparì, insieme a parte del paese di Mogno, in una devastante valanga nel 1986. Le drammatiche cause che hanno generato l'incarico hanno portato alla necessità di prestare particolare attenzione alla relazione dell'edificio con l'ambiente, alle tecniche costruttive con le quali lavorare, e all'espressione, sia fisica che simbolica, che doveva assumere l'insieme in un contesto naturale così sconvolgente. Botta ha scelto una costruzione composta da grandi muri di pietra, rinforzati da contrafforti, ed una leggera copertura in vetro. Questo contrasto materializza la fragilità dell'uomo davanti alla forza della natura, ma aspira anche a conferire all'individuo un luogo dove comunicare con dio a tu per tu. La pianta è guidata da forme geometriche semplici: un rettangolo inscritto in un'ellisse che nella copertura si trasforma in una circonferenza. Questa chiarezza compositiva è enfatizzata da un sistema costruttivo semplice che soddisfa la resistenza strutturale richiesta.

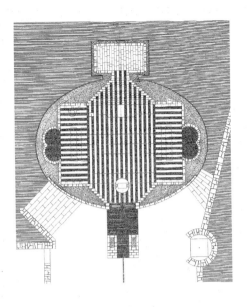

Plan   Grundriss
Niveau   Pianta

Longitudinal section   Längsschnitt
Section longitudinale   Sezione longitudinale

Cymbalista Synagogue

Location: Tel Aviv University, Tel Aviv, Israel
Date of construction: 1996–1998
Photographer: Pino Musi

The couple Paulette and Norbert Cymbalista commissioned Mario Botta for the construction of a synagogue at Tel Aviv university. Requirements for this project included that of an ideal space for prayer, reflection, and discussion. The synagogue and a room for conferences should deliver a space where the religious and the secular can co-exist. Consultation with the university authorities resulted in the choice of a small site on one corner of the terrain used by the students to meet in assembly. The new building stemming from these conditions would be perceivable as a student service feature. It is perhaps precisely the exactitude of Paulette and Norbert Cymbalista's requisites that will help Botta generate his simple, clear edifice: two functionally independent spaces whose interface is formal. The solution hit on is two towers brought into contact with each other by a ground floor containing the vestibule and the service areas. The square plan of the towers' bases develops upward, in the shape of two truncated cones culminating in circular roofs. The by no means ordinary proportion, blending with the sculpture of the façades, makes the edifice an important one on this university campus and evokes the spiritual memory of the community.

Le couple formé par Paulette et Norbert Cymbalista commanda à Mario Botta là construction d'une synagogue pour l'université de Tel Aviv. Le projet devait offrir un espace propre à la prière, à la réflexion et à la discussion, une synagogue et une salle de conférence, un espace permettant au religieux et au séculaire de vivre en bonne entente. Avec les autorités de l'université fut choisi un petit site, dans un des angles du terrain utilisé par les étudiants pour se réunir en assemblée. De cette forme, le nouvel édifice devait être perçu comme un équipement au service des étudiants. La précision des conditions requises par les Cymbalistas aida Botta à générer une construction simple et claire : deux espaces fonctionnellement indépendants mais formellement connectés. De là, l'idée de deux tours unies par un rez-de-chaussée abritant le hall et les services. Les bases carrées des tours se transforment avec leur élévation en deux cônes, culminant en deux toiture circulaires. Les proportions inhabituelles et les finitions sculpturales des façades convertissent l'édifice en un élément de sens au sein du campus universitaire, évoquant la mémoire spirituelle de la communauté.

Das Ehepaar Paulette und Norbert Cymbalista erteilte Mario Botta den Auftrag zum Bau einer Synagoge für die Universität von Tel Aviv. Der Entwurf sollte Räumlichkeiten zum Beten, Nachdenken und Diskutieren vorsehen. Es sollte mit einer Synagoge und einem Konferenzsaal ein Ort geschaffen werden, an dem Religiöses und Weltliches einträchtig nebeneinander bestehen können. In Abstimmung mit der Universität wurde als Bauplatz ein Bereich des Uni-Geländes ausgewählt, in dem sich die Studenten zu Versammlungen zusammenfinden. Damit wollte man sicherstellen, dass sie das neue Gebäude als eine Einrichtung für sich begreifen würden. Die genauen Vorgaben der Cymbalistas halfen Botta, einen einfachen, klaren Bau mit zwei funktional unabhängigen, doch formal miteinander verknüpften Teilen zu entwickeln. Die zwei Türme sind durch ein gemeinsames Erdgeschoss verbunden, in dem sich die Eingangshalle und die Diensträume befinden. Von quadratischen Grundrissen ausgehend entwickeln sich die beiden Türme zu umgedrehten Kegeln mit runden Dächern. Die ungewöhnlichen Proportionen und der skulpturale Fassadenschmuck haben die Synagoge zu einem wichtigen Gebäude auf dem Campus werden lassen, das die geistliche Erinnerung der Gemeinschaft wach hält.

I coniugi Paulette e Norbert Cymbalista incaricarono a Mario Botta la costruzione di una sinagoga nell'università di Tel Aviv. Il progetto doveva fornire uno spazio idoneo per pregare, riflettere e discutere; una sinagoga ed una sala per conferenze, un luogo dove religioso e profano potessero convivere. Insieme alle autorità universitarie è stato scelto un piccolo lotto in uno degli angoli del terreno che gli studenti utilizzano per riunirsi in assemblea. In questo modo, il nuovo edificio è avvertito come un impianto a servizio degli studenti. La chiarezza delle richieste dei Cymbalista ha aiutato Botta a dar vita ad una costruzione semplice e chiara: due spazi funzionalmente indipendenti ma collegati formalmente. In questo modo sono state ideate due torri unite da un piano terra dove sono situati l'ingresso ed i servizi. La base quadrata delle torri si trasforma, innalzandosi, in due coni che culminano con due rispettive coperture circolari. La proporzione insolita e le finiture scultoree delle facciate trasformano l'edificio in una costruzione significativa all'interno del campus universitario, che evoca la memoria spirituale della comunità.

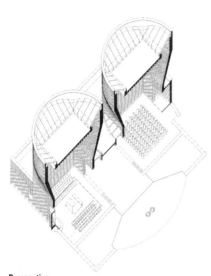

Perspective
Perspektivzeichnung
Perspective
Prospettiva

0   5   10

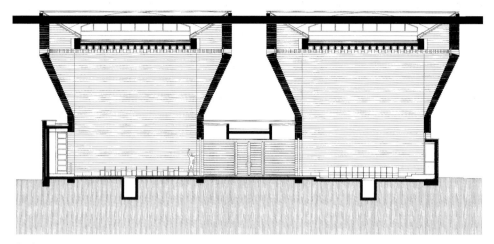

Section
Schnitt
Section
Sezione

0 5 10

Municipal Library

Location: Am Königswall, Dortmund, Germany
Date of construction: 1997–1999
Photographers: Markus Steur, Cornelia Suhan, Ralph Richter

Libraries today suffer a loss of identity due to the introduction of the new technologies and to the fact that, not infrequently, they fail to satisfy their users' practical needs. The concept on which Botta will base his project is that of underscoring the public dimension of the new building. He will thus divide the complex in two, with a rigid, straight-line body in front of the railroad track limiting the site on one side; and a transparent cone where he put the reading rooms, the consultation rooms, and those housing the computers. The solid-material façade is altered by thin vertical openings that break up the rhythm of the parallelepiped design. The double glass façade of the lightweight volume reduces to a skeleton of metal pieces that support the pre-stressed roof. Inside, Botta establishes a network of passageways and catwalks to interface with all of the spaces and floors of the whole. He thus empowers communication among the different services on offer. Dortmund has a library that rises up as a symbol of memory reconstruction: an investment in the language of developing the city's future.

Im Zeitalter der neuen Technologien können die Bibliotheken nicht immer alle praktischen Bedürfnisse ihrer Nutzer sofort befriedigen und leiden daher unter einem Identitätsverlust. Mario Botta wollte mit seinem Entwurf den öffentlichen Charakter des Gebäudes hervorheben. Der Bau ist in zwei Teile gegliedert: Ein starrer Riegel verläuft parallel zur Bahnlinie an der Grundstücksgrenze und ein transparenter konischer Baukörper nimmt die Lesesäle, Informationsbereiche und Computerarbeitsplätze auf. In die Fassade des Quaders sind schmale senkrechte Schlitze eingeschnitten, um ihre Gleichförmigkeit zu durchbrechen, während die doppelt verglaste Fassade des Publikumsbereichs aus einer Metallstruktur besteht, die das Dach stützt. Im Inneren verbindet ein Netz von Gängen und Stegen alle Ebenen und Bereiche miteinander und erleichtert die Kommunikation zwischen den verschiedenen Dienstleistungseinrichtungen. Die Stadtbibliothek von Dortmund gilt als ein Symbol der Rekonstruktion der Erinnerung und setzt zugleich auf die zukünftige Entwicklung der Stadt.

Les bibliothèques souffrent aujourd'hui d'une perte d'identité due à l'introduction des nouvelles technologies et au fait que, bien souvent, elles ne répondent pas aux nécessités pratiques de leurs usagers. Botta a fondé son projet sur un concept : détacher la dimension publique du nouvel édifice. Il a donc divisé le complexe en deux parties : un corps rigide et linéaire, devant la voie ferrée jouxtant le terrain, et un volume conique transparent, où ont été situées les salles de lecture, celles de consultation et celles accueillant les ordinateurs. La façade de la construction massive a été altérée par de fines ouvertures verticales qui rompent le rythme de la composition du parallélépipède, alors que la double façade vitrée du fin volume est constituée d'un squelette d'éléments métalliques qui supportent la toiture sous tension. À l'intérieur, un réseau de couloirs et de passerelles connecte ensemble tous les espaces et les niveaux, facilitant la communication entre les divers services. La bibliothèque de Dortmund se dresse en symbole de la reconstruction de la mémoire mais aussi comme un pari pour le développement futur de la ville.

Attualmente le biblioteche soffrono una perdita d'identità conseguente all'introduzione delle nuove tecnologie e al fatto che spesso non soddisfano le necessità pratiche degli utenti. Il concetto sul quale Botta ha basato il suo progetto è stato quello di evidenziare la dimensione pubblica del nuovo edificio, così che ha diviso il complesso in due parti: un corpo rigido e lineare davanti ai binari del treno confinanti col lotto, ed un volume conico trasparente dove sono situate le sale di lettura, quelle di consultazione e quelle che accolgono i computer. La facciata della costruzione massiccia è alterata da delle sottili aperture verticali che rompono il ritmo compositivo del parallelepipedo, mentre la doppia facciata vetrata del volume leggero è composta da uno scheletro di elementi metallici che sostengono la tensostruttura di copertura. All'interno, una rete di corridoi e passerelle collega tutti gli spazi e le piante del complesso, potenziando la comunicazione fra i diversi servizi. La biblioteca di Dortmund si erge come un simbolo della ricostruzione della memoria e come una sfida per lo sviluppo futuro della città.

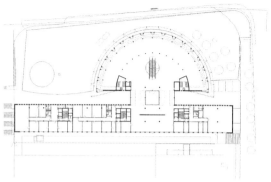

Second floor
Zweites Obergeschoss
Deuxième étage
Piano secondo

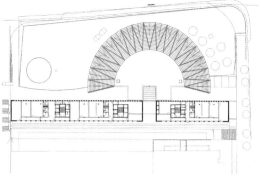

Fourth floor
Viertes Obergeschoss
Quatrième étage
Piano quarto

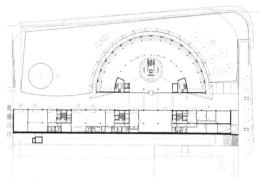

Ground floor
Erdgeschoss
Rez-de-chaussée
Piano terra

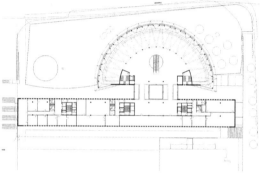

First floor
Erstes Obergeschoss
Premier étage
Piano primo

0   5   10

Villa Redaelli

Location: Bernareggio, Italy
Date of construction: 1996–2000
Photographer: Pino Musi

The project we see here was brought to life by means of a study of the urban conditions, the building code, and the interpretation of the site within its context. The complex was not lacking a picturesque backdrop, raised on a meadow some ways outside the town of Bernareggio, on the skirts of the foothills of the Alps. The program was planned to include the construction of ten semi-detached houses and a villa. The dwellings were drawn up as if in a large wall, one on the shoulder of the road linking the town center with the Alps themselves. And in spite of the fact that it takes on the appearance of a large, straight wall, the built project of the villa is in fact a sectioned cylinder. On the circular part, which gives onto the landscape, the residence complex was successively cut out of recesses in the façades and the opening of cavities designed to separate some of the houses from others. The windows providing light and ventilation to the domestic spaces open out from these big slices, leaving the main front smooth, with an eastern orientation, and emphasizing the solid look of the complex. The villa was set at one end of the whole to stand its own ground in counterpoint with the rest of the intervention.

Der Planung dieses Projektes gingen umfassende städtebauliche sowie baurechtliche Studien zum Grundstück und seiner Umgebung voraus. Der Komplex entstand auf einer Wiese in der malerischen Umgebung von Bernareggio am Fuße der Alpen. Das Programm sah den Bau von zehn Reihenhäusern und einer Villa vor. Die Reihenhäuser wurden als eine große Mauer am Rande der Straße gestaltet, die den Ortskern mit den Alpen verbindet. Doch obwohl es sich um eine langgezogene Wand zu handeln scheint, hat der Baukörper der Villa eigentlich die Form eines angeschnittenen Zylinders. Die zur Landschaft gewandte, abgerundete Seite ist durch Rücksprünge in der Fassade und tiefere Einschnitte gegliedert, die die einzelnen Reihenhäuser voneinander trennen. Die Fenster zur Beleuchtung und Belüftung der Wohnungen gehen auf diese größeren Einschnitte hinaus, so dass die nach Osten liegende Mauer glatt bleibt und der solide Eindruck der Anlage noch unterstrichen wird. Die separate Villa wurde gleichsam als Gegenpol an ein Ende dieses Komplexes gesetzt.

L'emplacement du projet a été déterminé suite à l'étude des conditions urbaines, des normes en vigueur ainsi que de l'interprétation du terrain et de son contexte. L'ensemble voit le jour dans un cadre pittoresque, une prairie des alentours de la ville de Bernareggio, au pied des Préalpes. Le programme comprenait la construction de dix maisons adossées et d'une villa. Les demeures ont été projetées comme s'il s'agissait d'un grand mur, d'une muraille au bord de la route reliant le centre de la ville et les Alpes. Malgré la similarité avec une grande paroi rectiligne, la construction de la villa occupe un volume cylindrique sectionné. La partie circulaire, s'ouvrant au paysage, accueille l'immeuble scindé à l'aide de retraits dans la façade et des ouvertures de cavités conçues pour séparer les maisons les unes des autres. Les fenêtres apportent lumière et ventilation aux espaces privés et s'ouvrent sur ses fissures amples, préservant le lissé de la fermeture principale, orientée à l'Est, et soulignant l'aspect solide de l'ensemble. La villa a été située à l'un des extrêmes et s'élève en contrepoint de l'ensemble de l'intervention.

La composizione progettuale è sorta dallo studio delle condizioni urbanistiche, della normativa vigente, e dalle caratteristiche del lotto e del suo intorno. Il complesso è stato costruito in una cornice pittoresca, in una prateria alla periferia della località di Bernareggio, ai piedi delle montagne che precedono le Alpi. Il programma comprendeva la costruzione di dieci case e di una villa. Gli alloggi sono stati progettati come se si trattasse di un grande muro, una muraglia al bordo della strada che collega il centro dell'abitato con le Alpi. Nonostante appaia come una grande parete rettilinea, la costruzione della villa occupa un volume cilindrico sezionato. Nella parte circolare, che si apre verso il paesaggio, l'immobile è stato reciso con dei rientri nelle facciate e con l'apertura di cavità progettate per separare una casa dall'altra. Le finestre, che forniscono luce e ventilazione agli spazi domestici, si aprono su queste grandi fenditure, lasciando liscia la parete principale orientata ad est ed enfatizzando l'aspetto solido del complesso. La villa è stata collocata in una delle estremità e si innalza come contrappunto di tutto l'intervento.

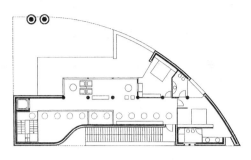

Second floor Zweites Obergeschoss
Deuxième étage Piano secondo

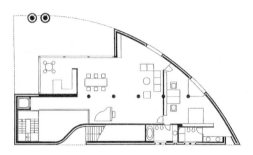

First floor Erstes Obergeschoss
Premier étage Piano primo

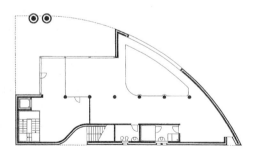

Ground floor Erdgeschoss
Rez-de-chaussée Piano terra

0 5 10

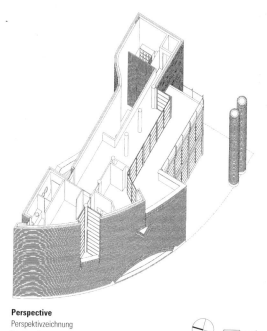

Perspective
Perspektivzeichnung
Perspective
Prospettiva

0 5 10

Dürrenmatt Center

Location: Chemin Pertuis-du-Sault 74, Neuchâtel, Switzerland
Date of construction: 1997–2000
Photographer: Pino Musi

After the death of the versatile writer, Friedrich Dürrenmatt, his wife decided to share the artist's valuable legacy. She commissioned Mario Botta with the construction of a museum to house the drawings and other objects that had belonged to Dürrenmatt. The center was to be a place that would express the values of this unique personality, a building that would reflect the style of his strong spirit. As an admirer of the Swiss writer, Botta was ready to undertake a project that would do homage to his work. Raised on a mountain site, the center comprises a tower and a large two-story "baseboard" that serves as an exhibition space. The roof acts as a mirador onto the panoramic views of the landscape. The visitor to this center enters it by a small vestibule between the tower and the Dürrenmatt family house which had already been used as a library. A stairway leads to the exhibition room that is formed by a large, curved concrete wall, its exterior covered in pieces of slate, the same material that has been used as flooring. From the project's origins, an intimate complex was conceived. It was to have little interference from outside, and this feature led to the somewhat unordinary recourse of limiting the number of windows.

Nach dem Tode des vielseitigen Schriftstellers Friedrich Dürrenmatt beschloss seine Witwe, den wertvollen Nachlass der Allgemeinheit zugänglich zu machen und beauftragte Mario Botta mit der Planung eines Museums für die Zeichnungen und anderen Gegenstände aus dem Besitz des Autors. Das Gebäude sollte dabei zugleich auch den Geist des Dramatikers und die Wertvorstellungen seiner einzigartigen Persönlichkeit widerspiegeln. Botta war sehr angetan von der Vorstellung, dem von ihm verehrten Schweizer Autor nun selbst eine Hommage darbringen zu können. Das Dürrenmatt-Zentrum liegt auf bergigem Gelände. Es besteht aus einem Turm und einem zweigeschossigen Sockelbau für Ausstellungen, von dessen Dach aus man die Landschaft betrachten kann. Die Besucher betreten den Komplex über eine kleine Vorhalle, die zwischen dem Turm und dem Haus der Dürrenmatts liegt, das schon länger als Bibliothek dient. Eine Treppe führt in den Ausstellungsraum, der von einer großen gekrümmten Betonwand beherrscht wird. Von außen ist diese Wand mit Schieferplatten verkleidet, wie sie auch bei den Fußböden Verwendung fanden. Es war von Anfang an klar, dass ein intimer, vor äußeren Einflüssen geschützter Ort geschaffen werden sollte. Daher wurde auf Fensteröffnungen fast ganz verzichtet.

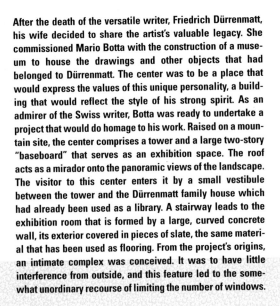

Après le décès de Friedrich Dürrenmatt, écrivain aux multiples facettes, son épouse décida de partager son précieux legs artistique. Elle commanda à Mario Botta la construction d'un musée afin d'accueillir les dessins et autres objets de Dürrenmatt : un endroit qui saurait exprimer les valeurs de sa personnalité unique, un édifice qui donnerait forme à son esprit. Le projet enthousiasma Botta, déjà admirateur de l'œuvre de l'auteur suisse, passionné à l'idée de pouvoir lui rendre hommage à travers son propre travail. Situé sur un terrain montagneux, le centre est formé d'une tour et d'une vaste module sur deux étages abritant les expositions et dont la toiture offre un mirador pour le paysage. Le visiteur accède au complexe par une petit hall situé entre la tour et la maison de la famille Dürrenmatt, utilisée depuis déjà longtemps comme bibliothèque. Un escalier mène à la salle d'exposition, l'édification étant confiée à un grand mur curviligne en béton, couvert à l'extérieur en ardoises, aussi utilisées pour revêtir le sol. Dès le départ, le lieu a été pensé pour l'intimité : les interférences avec l'extérieur étant limitées par l'ouverture réduite des fenêtres.

Dopo la morte del versatile scrittore Friedrich Dürrenmatt, la moglie decise di spartire la sua preziosa eredità artistica ed incaricò Mario Botta della costruzione di un museo che ospitasse i disegni ed altri oggetti di Dürrenmatt, un luogo che esprimesse i valori della sua personalità unica, un edificio che potesse dar forma al suo spirito. Il progetto entusiasmò Botta, che già ammirava l'opera dell'autore svizzero, e lo stimolò a rendergli omaggio col proprio lavoro. Situato su un terreno montuoso, il centro è formato da una torre e da un grande basamento di due piani che accoglie le mostre, la cui copertura agisce come veranda sul paesaggio. Il visitatore accede al complesso attraverso un piccolo ingresso situato tra la torre e la casa della famiglia Dürrenmatt, che viene utilizzata già da tempo come biblioteca. Una scalinata porta alla sala mostre, costituita da un gran muro curvo di cemento, coperto all'esterno con elementi di ardesia che vengono utilizzati anche nel pavimento. Fin dal principio si è pensato in un luogo intimo, con poche interferenze dell'esterno, per cui le aperture sono state ridotte al minimo.

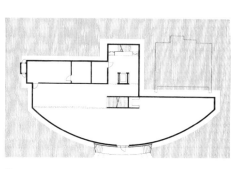

Basement
Souterrain
Sous-sol
Piano interrato

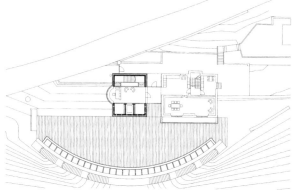

Ground floor
Erdgeschoss
Rez-de-chaussée
Piano terra

0 5 10

National Sports Center

Location: Tenero, Ticino, Switzerland
Date of construction: 1998–2001
Photographer: Enrico Cano

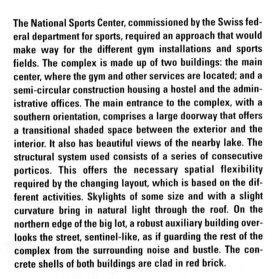

The National Sports Center, commissioned by the Swiss federal department for sports, required an approach that would make way for the different gym installations and sports fields. The complex is made up of two buildings: the main center, where the gym and other services are located; and a semi-circular construction housing a hostel and the administrative offices. The main entrance to the complex, with a southern orientation, comprises a large doorway that offers a transitional shaded space between the exterior and the interior. It also has beautiful views of the nearby lake. The structural system used consists of a series of consecutive porticos. This offers the necessary spatial flexibility required by the changing layout, which is based on the different activities. Skylights of some size and with a slight curvature bring in natural light through the roof. On the northern edge of the big lot, a robust auxiliary building overlooks the street, sentinel-like, as if guarding the rest of the complex from the surrounding noise and bustle. The concrete shells of both buildings are clad in red brick.

Dieses Projekt, bei dem es sich um einen Auftrag des schweizerischen Bundesamtes für Sport handelt, sollte verschiedene Sport- und Gymnastikanlagen umfassen. Der Komplex besteht aus einem Hauptgebäude mit der Sporthalle und sonstigen Einrichtungen und einem halbkreisförmigen Nebengebäude mit einem Hostel und Verwaltungsräumen. Der Eingang zum Hauptgebäude öffnet sich nach Süden: Ein großzügiger Portikus, der einen schattigen Übergangsbereich zwischen Innen und Außen darstellt und von dem aus man eine herrliche Aussicht auf einen nahen See genießt. Das verwendete Konstruktionsprinzip von aufeinanderfolgenden Pfeilern erlaubt eine flexible Gestaltung und Nutzung des Raums für sportliche Aktivitäten. Durch große Oberlichter in den leicht gewölbten Decken erhalten die Räume reichlich natürliches Licht. Im nördlichen Teil der Anlage erhebt sich das robuste zweite Gebäude, gleich neben der Straße, so als wollte es das Areal vor Lärm und Störungen aus der Umgebung abschirmen. Beide Gebäude des Komplexes tragen eine Verkleidung aus rötlichem Backstein über der Betonstruktur.

Ce projet, une commande du ministère fédéral suisse des sports, devait accueillir diverses installations destinées à la pratique du sport et de la gymnastique. Le complexe présente deux bâtiments : le principal où se trouvent le gymnase et les autres services ; et une construction semi-circulaire qui abrite une maison d'hôte et les bureaux administratifs. L'entrée principale du complexe, orientée vers le sud, dispose d'un grand portique offrant un espace de transition ombré entre l'extérieur et l'intérieur du centre. Elle jouit en outre de superbes vues sur le lac, tout proche. Le système structurel de cette construction présente une série de portiques consécutifs offrant la souplesse spatiale nécessaire à la disposition changeante des activités. De grandes claires-voies inscrites dans la toiture, légèrement voûtée, fournissent une lumière naturelle abondante. Dans la partie nord du terrain, le bâtiment auxiliaire se dresse solidement, du côté rue, comme s'il s'agissait de protéger le reste du complexe du bruit et de l'agitation environnants. À l'extérieur, le béton structurel des deux édifices a été revêtu de briques rouges.

Questo progetto, incaricato dal ministero federale svizzero per lo sport, doveva accogliere diversi impianti per la pratica dello sport e della ginnastica. Il complesso è composto da due edifici: quello principale dove si trovano la palestra ed i servizi ed una costruzione semicircolare che ospita un ostello e gli uffici dell'amministrazione. L'entrata principale al complesso, orientata a sud, avviene attraverso un grande portico che offre uno spazio ombreggiato di transizione tra l'esterno e l'interno del centro e che gode anche di splendide vedute del lago vicino. Il sistema strutturale di questa costruzione è composto da una serie di portici consecutivi che offrono la necessaria flessibilità spaziale, richiesta dalla disposizione mutevole delle attività. Dei grandi lucernari inseriti nella copertura a leggera volta forniscono abbondante luce naturale. Nella zona nord del lotto, la costruzione accessoria si eleva robusta accanto alla strada, come se dovesse proteggere il resto del complesso dal rumore e dall'animazione circostante. All'esterno il cemento della struttura di entrambe le costruzioni è stato rivestito con mattoni rossi.

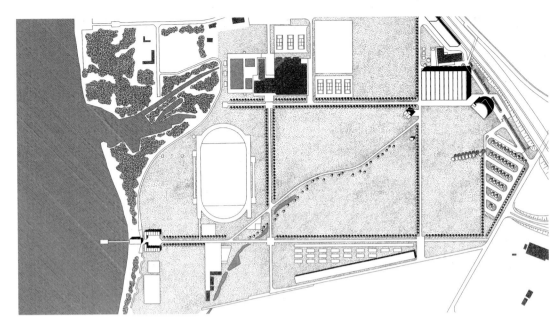

Plan
Grundriss
Niveau
Pianta

0 5 10

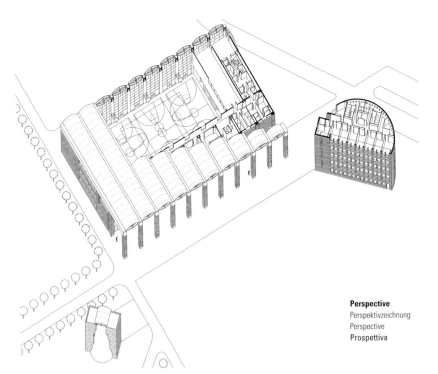

Perspective
Perspektivzeichnung
Perspective
Prospettiva

Noah's Ark Sculpture Garden

Location: Zoological Garden, Jerusalem, Israel
Date of construction: 1999–2001
Photographer: Pino Musi

Artist Niki de Saint Phalle proposed doing this collaboration with Mario Botta. It is the creation of a Noah's Ark inside the zoo in Jerusalem. Botta was very enthusiastic and accepted. He had, he confessed, since childhood marveled at the legend. The project was undertaken with something of the same fascination shown by children when they are involved in challenging activities. It is interesting to note, however, that the working philosophy of these two creators is very different: fantasy, color, irrationality are in the world of Niki de Saint Phalle, contrasting with the plainness, the monochromatism, and the order ruling the works of Botta. Yet there was no conflict, and the two contributions compliment each other, generating a functional, artistic, poetic space. The ark itself, designed by Botta in Jerusalem stone, forms an integral part of the playground equipment for kids, mostly a large cavity lighted by a big skylight. Outside are imaginative sculptures of animals painted by Niki de Saint Phalle in intense colors contrasting with the cool tones of the stone and the greenery of the park environs.

Die Künstlerin Niki de Saint Phalle schlug Mario Botta vor, mit ihr zusammen an der Errichtung einer Arche Noah für den Zoologischen Garten von Jerusalem zu arbeiten. Botta nahm die Einladung gerne an, weil er nach eigener Auskunft schon als Kind von der Geschichte Noahs fasziniert gewesen sei. Er begann das Projekt daher mit fast kindlicher Begeisterung. Die Arbeitsstile der beiden Künstler sind zwar sehr verschieden – die Fantasie, Farbenpracht und Irrationalität Niki de Saint Phalles stehen zu der nüchternen, monochromen Ordnung der Werke Mario Bottas in scharfem Gegensatz –, doch die Zusammenarbeit gelang und die Beiträge beider verschmolzen zu einem funktionalen, kunstvollen und poetischen Gesamtwerk. Die Arche ist einer der Spielplätze für Kinder im Zoo. Botta gestaltete sie aus Jerusalemer Stein wie eine Höhle, die durch ein großes Oberlicht erhellt wird. Die leuchtenden Farben der in den Außenanlagen aufgestellten fantasievollen Tierfiguren von Niki de Saint Phalle bilden zu dem gedeckten Ton des Steins und dem Grün der Vegetation einen lebhaften Kontrast.

L'artiste Niki de Saint Phalle a proposé à Mario Botta de coopérer avec elle pour construire une arche de Noé dans le parc accueillant le zoo de Jérusalem. Enchanté, Botta a accepté, confessant que depuis son enfance la légende l'avait émerveillé. Il s'affaira au projet avec la même passion qu'un enfant face à un nouveau défi. Bien que les philosophies de travail des deux créateurs soient très distinctes – la fantaisie, la couleur, l'irrationnel de Niki de Saint Phalle contrastent avec la sobriété, le monochromatisme et l'ordre régissant les œuvres de Botta – la coopération ne connut aucun conflit et les deux contributions purent se compléter, donnant vie à un espace fonctionnel, artistique et poétique. L'arche, conçue en pierre de Jérusalem par Botta, fait partie intégrante des équipements de loisirs des enfants. Elle propose une vaste cavité illuminée par une grande claire-voie. Contrastant avec le ton doux de la pierre et le vert du parc, des sculptures imaginatives d'animaux aux couleurs intenses, peintes par Niki de Saint Phalle ont été disposées sur l'extérieur de l'arche.

Fu l'artista Niki de Saint Phalle a proporre a Mario Botta di collaborare con lei nella costruzione di un'arca di Noè nel parco che ospita il giardino zoologico di Gerusalemme. Botta accettò entusiasta, confessando che fin da bambino l'aveva meravigliato la leggenda dell'arca, ed affrontò il progetto con lo stesso entusiasmo che sentono i bambini davanti alle sfide. Nonostante il fatto che la filosofia di lavoro dei due creatori fosse molto differente – la fantasia, la vivacità, l'irrazionalità di Niki de Saint Phalle contrasta con la sobrietà, il monocromatismo e l'ordine che regge le opere di Botta – non ci fu alcun conflitto e i due apporti si sono complementati generando uno spazio funzionale, artistico e poetico. L'arca, progettata da Botta in pietra di Gerusalemme, forma parte integrante dell'impianto ludico per i bambini ed è composta da un'ampia cavità illuminata da un gran lucernario. All'esterno sono state collocate le fantasiose sculture degli animali che Niki de Saint Phalle ha dipinto con colori intensi che contrastano col tono soave della pietra e col verde del parco.

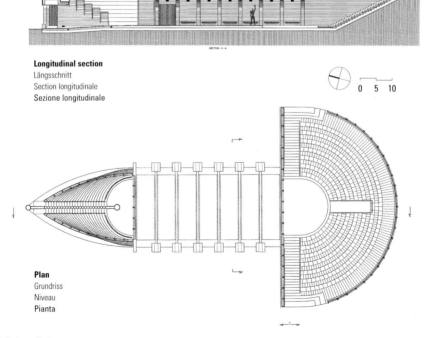

Longitudinal section
Längsschnitt
Section longitudinale
Sezione longitudinale

0 5 10

Plan
Grundriss
Niveau
Pianta

National Bank of Greece

Location: Eolou and Sofokleous Street, Athens, Greece
Date of construction: 1999–2001
Photographer: Pino Musi

Already in the 1970s, the administration building of the NBG was too small for its needs. Taking advantage of the Bank's centenary in 1998, a competition was offered and Mario Botta won it. The new proposal for the administration building was limited by the requirement that the architecture had to go up adjacent to the main building, right in the historical center of Athens. As the project opened, however, relevant archaeological remains were discovered, and this altered the design's development. The decision was taken to give these deposits special attention and convert the ground floor of the new edifice into a large public space that would serve as a platform from which to view the ruins. A large two-storey opening with a glass floor and metal walkways became the ideal framework for admiring the past of the city of Athens. In addition to this, a spectacular skylight flooded this inner patio with light. Thus, the peculiar setting of the piece, slotted between historical neo-classical buildings, led the architect to conceive a symmetrical main façade. This is made up of simple geometrical forms and a layer of sand-colored travertine. The flooring inside is of black granite and wood.

Das alte Gebäude der griechischen Nationalbank war bereits in den 1970er Jahren zu klein geworden. Doch erst 1998 wurde aus Anlass des hundertjährigen Bestehens der Einrichtung ein internationaler Architektenwettbewerb zur Errichtung eines Neubaus ausgelobt, den Mario Botta gewann. Der neue Baukörper sollte neben dem Hauptgebäude im historischen Zentrum Athens errichtet werden. Gleich zu Beginn der Bauarbeiten wurden bedeutende archäologische Entdeckungen gemacht, was zur Abänderung des Entwurfs führte. Es wurde beschlossen, den Bodenfunden besondere Aufmerksamkeit zu widmen und das Erdgeschoss des Neubaus als einen weitläufigen öffentlichen Raum zu gestalten, der die Geschichte der Stadt erlebbar macht. Ein großer zweistöckiger Bau mit gläsernen Fußböden und Metallstegen wurde errichtet, von denen aus die Besucher die Ruinen sehen können. Ein eindrucksvolles Oberlicht erhellt diesen Innenhof. Die städtebauliche Situation – der Neubau steht zwischen zwei klassizistischen Gebäuden – bewog den Architekten, eine aus einfachen Formen zusammengesetzte, symmetrische Hauptfassade zu entwerfen, die mit sandfarbenen Travertinplatten verkleidet wurde. Die Fußböden im Inneren sind aus schwarzem Granit bzw. Holz.

Depuis les années soixante-dix du XXème siècle, la Banque nationale de Grèce vivait à l'étroit dans son siège social. Le centenaire de l'institution, en 1998, offrait donc l'occasion de convoquer un concours international pour la construction d'un nouveau bâtiment remporté par Mario Botta. La nouvelle proposition devait s'ériger au côté de l'édifice principal, au cœur de l'Athènes historique. À l'orée du projet, la découverte de vestiges archéologiques d'importance altéra le développement de l'ensemble. Une attention spéciale devait être prêtée à l'objet trouvé. Le rez-de-chaussée du nouvel édifice se voyait transformé en un vaste espace public, servant de plate-forme d'observation des ruines. Un grand vide de deux niveaux, comportant un sol vitré et des passerelles métalliques, proposait le cadre parfait afin d'admirer le passé de la cité. En outre, une claire-voie spectaculaire inonde de lumière le patio intérieur. L'emplacement particulier de l'œuvre, entre des édifices historiques classique, a suggéré à l'architecte la conception d'une façade principale symétrique, composée de formes géométriques simples et de plaques de travertine aux tons sable. À l'intérieur, les revêtements s'habillent de granite noir et de bois.

Fin dagli anni settanta del XX° secolo, la sede della Banca Nazionale Greca era diventata insufficiente, per cui si è approfittato il centenario dell'istituzione, nel 1998, per convocare un concorso internazionale che ha vinto Mario Botta. La nuova proposta doveva essere costruita accanto all'edificio principale, nel centro storico di Atene. Appena cominciato l'intervento furono scoperti dei resti archeologici rilevanti che alterarono lo sviluppo del progetto. Si decise di prestare una particolare attenzione alla zona archeologica e trasformare il piano terra della costruzione in un grande spazio pubblico che servisse da piattaforma per osservare le rovine. Un grande vuoto di due piani, con pavimento in vetro e passerelle metalliche, è stato trasformato nella cornice idonea per ammirare il passato della città. Uno spettacolare lucernario inonda di luce questo cortile interno. La ubicazione dell'opera, collocata tra edifici classici, ha portato l'architetto a concepire una facciata principale simmetrica, composta da forme geometriche semplici e rivestimento in travertino di un tono color sabbia. All'interno, i pavimenti sono di granito nero e di legno.

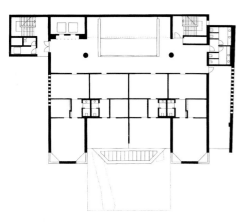

Second floor
Zweites Obergeschoss
Deuxième étage
Piano secondo

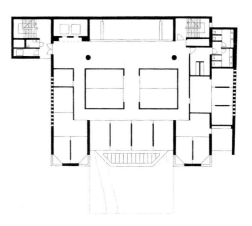

Fourth floor
Viertes Obergeschoss
Quatrième étage
Piano quarto

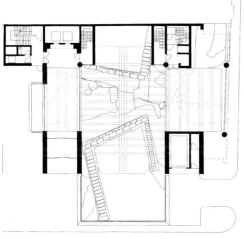

Ground floor
Erdgeschoss
Rez-de-chaussée
Piano terra

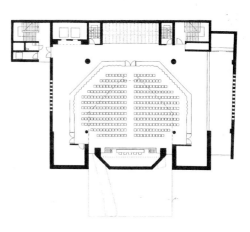

First floor
Erstes Obergeschoss
Premier étage
Piano primo

0 5 10

Harting Offices

Location: Simeonscarré, Minden, Germany
Date of construction: 2000–2001
Photographers: Rainer Hofmann, Enrico Cano

The project for the technology group Harting was raised in the historical center of Minden; hence, from the very outset, those contextual buildings already standing comprised a kind of knot that had to be untied—perhaps the main kernel of the entire work. The modern language is slated to contrast and play up the urban environment through the use of traditional materials such as natural stone. The end product is harmonious contextualization. In addition to all of this, the edifice has to meet certain technical requirements and functional ones in keeping with offices associated with today's fast-paced world. It also had to satisfy client needs: to materialize the firm's spirit via the expression of concepts like security, constancy, solidity. In the light of all these premises, Mario Botta conceived something elliptical showing great presence, its main front flanked by two towers and the ellipse itself topped by a steep roof. Special emphasis here on the ecology: the careful interiors use materials yielding optimal potentials that reduce the artificial energy load and plan for the different seasons of the year. Solar rays are factored in to the maximum. Their main function is to light the place and to improve the air conditioning.

Der Bürokomplex für den Technologie-Konzern Harting befindet sich im Stadtzentrum von Minden. Daher wurde schon bei Beginn der Planung großer Wert auf die Beziehung zu den benachbarten Altbauten gelegt. Botta entschied sich für eine moderne Formensprache, die in bewusstem Kontrast zur Umgebung steht, doch die gewählten Materialien, wie etwa der traditionelle Naturstein der Fassadenverkleidung, sorgen für einen harmonischen Gesamteindruck. Außerdem musste das Gebäude den technischen und funktionalen Anforderungen an moderne Bürotechnik entsprechen und schließlich den Ansprüchen des Bauherrn genügen, also den Charakter des Unternehmens herausstellen, für den Begriffe wie Sicherheit, Beständigkeit und Zuverlässigkeit stehen. Botta löste die Aufgabe mit einem auffälligen ellipsenförmigen Baukörper mit stark geneigtem Dach, dessen Hauptfassade zwei Türme flankieren. Von großer Bedeutung waren auch ökologische Aspekte: Im Inneren wurden äußerst leistungsfähige Materialien eingesetzt, die den Energieverbrauch zu allen Jahreszeiten minimieren sollen. Die Sonnenstrahlen werden im größtmöglichen Umfang zur Beleuchtung und Klimaverbesserung im Gebäude genutzt.

Le projet des bureaux pour l'enterprise technologique Harting est situé dans le centre historique de Minden. Ainsi, dès le départ, la relation avec les anciens immeubles voisins fut un des aspects les plus étudiés. Un langage moderne a été choisi, contrastant avec l'environnement et le mettant en valeur. Les matériaux traditionnels, ainsi la pierre naturelle, ont été sélectionnés afin de créer un contexte harmonieux. D'un autre côté, la construction devait respecter les exigences techniques et fonctionnelles propres des bureaux contemporains, tout en satisfaisant aux impératifs des clients : matérialiser l'esprit de la société en exprimant des concepts comme la sécurité, la constance et la solidité. En fonction de ces prémisses, Mario Botta a conçu un volume elliptique à la présence imposante flanqué, sur la façade principale, de deux tours et couronné d'une toiture très inclinée. L'accent a tout spécialement été porté sur les aspects écologiques. Ainsi les matériaux employés à l'intérieur offrent-ils des prestations optimum réduisant les coûts en énergie artificielle entre les diverses saisons de l'année. Les rayons du soleil sont rentabilisés au maximum, mis à profit pour illuminer mais aussi améliorer la circulation de l'air.

Gli uffici per la compagnia tecnologica Harting sono situati nel centro storico di Minden, il che ha reso il rapporto con gli antichi edifici limitrofi, fin dal principio, uno degli aspetti più studiati del progetto. È stato scelto un linguaggio moderno, per creare contrasto e risaltare l'intorno urbanistico, e sono stati scelti dei materiali tradizionali, come la pietra naturale, per creare un contesto armonioso. Oltre a ciò, la costruzione doveva adempiere alle esigenze tecniche e funzionali proprie degli uffici attuali, ed anche soddisfare le necessità dei clienti: dar corpo allo spirito della ditta mediante l'espressione di concetti come la sicurezza, la costanza e la solidità. Attraverso queste premesse, Mario Botta ha concepito un volume ellittico di forte presenza, fiancheggiato, nella facciata principale, da due torri, e coronato da una copertura fortemente inclinata. È stata conferita un'enfasi speciale agli aspetti ecologici. Così i materiali utilizzati all'interno offrono delle ottime prestazioni che riducono il consumo di energia elettrica nelle diverse stagioni dell'anno. La radiazione solare dà il massimo rendimento ed è utilizzata sia per illuminare che per migliorare le condizioni dell'aria.

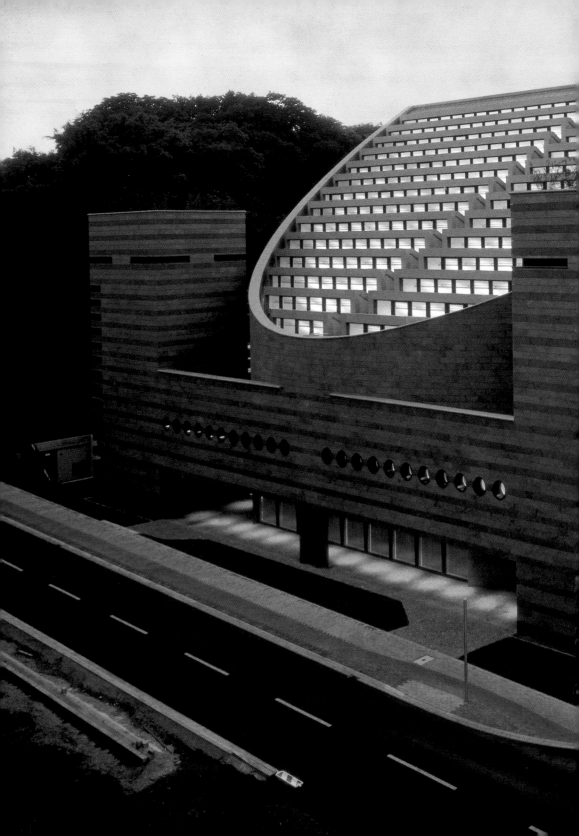

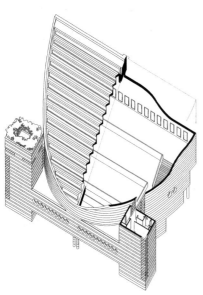

Perspective
Perspektivzeichnung
Perspective
Prospettiva

0 5 10

Museum of Modern Art of Rovereto and Trento

Location: Corso Bettini 43, Rovereto, Italy
Date of construction: 1996–2002
Photographers: Enrico Cano, Pino Musi

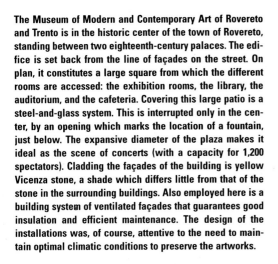

The Museum of Modern and Contemporary Art of Rovereto and Trento is in the historic center of the town of Rovereto, standing between two eighteenth-century palaces. The edifice is set back from the line of façades on the street. On plan, it constitutes a large square from which the different rooms are accessed: the exhibition rooms, the library, the auditorium, and the cafeteria. Covering this large patio is a steel-and-glass system. This is interrupted only in the center, by an opening which marks the location of a fountain, just below. The expansive diameter of the plaza makes it ideal as the scene of concerts (with a capacity for 1,200 spectators). Cladding the façades of the building is yellow Vicenza stone, a shade which differs little from that of the stone in the surrounding buildings. Also employed here is a building system of ventilated façades that guarantees good insulation and efficient maintenance. The design of the installations was, of course, attentive to the need to maintain optimal climatic conditions to preserve the artworks.

Das Museum für moderne und zeitgenössische Kunst von Trient und Rovereto liegt in der historischen Altstadt von Rovereto zwischen zwei Stadtpalästen aus dem 18. Jahrhundert. Der Bau ist von der Straße zurückversetzt. Von einem großen Platz aus gelangt man zu den verschiedenen Einrichtungen des Museums: den Ausstellungsräumen, der Bibliothek, dem Veranstaltungssaal und der Cafeteria. Dieser große Innenhof wird von einer Konstruktion aus Metallprofilen mit großen Glasplatten überdacht. Nur in der Mitte bleibt eine Öffnung, genau über einem Brunnen. Die großzügigen Dimensionen dieser Piazza erlauben die Nutzung für Veranstaltungen mit bis zu 1.200 Besuchern wie etwa Konzerte. Die Fassaden des Gebäudekomplexes sind mit gelbem Stein aus Vicenza verkleidet, dessen Farbton den Steinfassaden der umstehenden Häuser gleicht. Ein spezielles Ventilationssystem in den Fassaden gewährleistet eine gute Isolierung und erleichtert die Instandhaltung. Bei der Gestaltung der Innenbereiche musste besonders auf die für den Erhalt der Kunstwerke erforderlichen optimalen klimatischen Bedingungen Rücksicht genommen werden.

Le musée d'art moderne et contemporain de Trente et Rovereto est situé dans le centre historique du Rovereto, entre deux palais du XVIIIème siècle. L'édifice est en retrait par rapport aux façades de la rue et est doté d'une grande place, permettant d'accéder aux différentes parties du musée : les salles d'exposition, la bibliothèque, l'auditorium et la cafétéria. Ce grand patio est couvert par un système de pièces métalliques soutenant de grands panneaux vitrés, interrompus uniquement en leur centre, où un grand trou dans la toiture correspond avec une source située juste en dessous. L'amplitude de la place lui permet de jouer les scènes de concert, offrant une capacité de 1.200 spectateurs. Les façades de l'édifice sont recouvertes de pierre jaune de Vicenza, à la tonalité semblable à celle des constructions voisines. Le système architectural de la façade est ventilé afin d'assurer un bon isolement et un entretien efficace. La conception des installations a été minutieuse, du fait de la nécessité de préserver des conditions d'environnement optimales pour garantir la conservation des œuvres.

Il museo d'arte moderna e contemporanea di Trento e Rovereto è situato nel centro storico della località, tra due palazzi del XVIII° secolo. L'edificio è arretrato rispetto alle facciate sulla strada, ed è composto da una grande piazza dalla quale si accede alle diverse parti del museo: le sale d'esposizione, la biblioteca, l'auditorium e il bar. Questo grande cortile è coperto da un sistema di profilati metallici che sostengono grandi pannelli di vetro interrotti, solo nel centro, da un foro nella copertura che corrisponde ad una fontana situata giusto al di sotto. L'ampio diametro della piazza permette di utilizzarla come scenario per concerti, con una capacità per 1.200 spettatori. Le facciate della costruzione sono rivestite di pietra gialla di Vicenza, di una tonalità simile a quella della pietra degli edifici circostanti. Per garantire un buon isolamento ed un'efficace manutenzione, è stato realizzato un sistema costruttivo con facciata ventilata. Il progetto degli impianti è stato studiato con particolare attenzione, per la necessità di mantenere delle condizioni climatiche ottimali che salvaguardassero le opere d'arte.

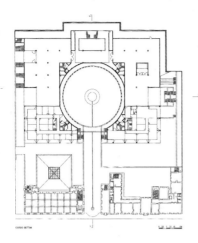

First floor
Erstes Obergeschoss
Premier étage
Piano primo

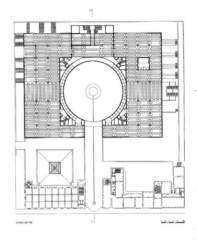

Second floor
Zweites Obergeschoss
Deuxième étage
Piano secondo

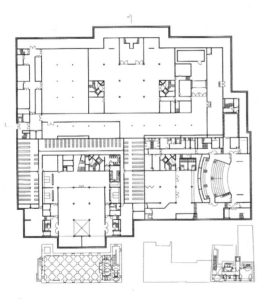

Basement
Souterrain
Sous-sol
Piano interrato

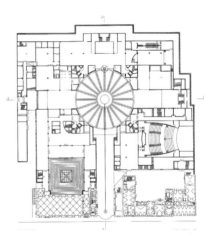

Ground floor
Erdgeschoss
Rez-de-chaussée
Piano terra

Chronology 1990–2002

1990	National Sports Center, Tenero, Ticino, Switzerland.
	Chapel of Saint Mary of the Angels, Alpe Foppa-Tamaro, Ticino, Switzerland.
	Commercial building in Vimercate, Italy.
	Administration Building Editorial La Provincia, Como, Italy.
	Casino, Campione d'Italia, Italy.
	Offices and Residences La Fortezza, Maastricht, the Netherlands.
	Carpets 483 Nero, 483 Verde Rame, Marenza, La cattedrale for Lantal Textiles.
	Chair Botta 91 for Alias.
	Administration building in Merate, Italy.
1991	Industrial Building Thermoselect in Fondotoce-Verbania, Italy.
	Home for children in Rajsko, Poland.
	Piazzale alla Valle Center, Mendrisio, Switzerland.
	Villa Redaelli, Bernareggio, Italy.
1992	San Francisco Museum of Modern Art, San Francisco, California, USA.
	Screen Nilla Rosa for Alias.
	Library Werner Oechslin, Einsiedeln, Switzerland.
	Church of Saint John the Baptist, Mogno, Ticino, Switzerland.
	Vase for Cleto Munari.
	Courtyard roof in Locarno, Switzerland.
	Residences in Monte Carasso, Ticino, Switzerland.
	Set design for the "Nutcracker" at the Opernhaus, Zurich, Switzerland.
	Home for eldery, Novazzano, Switzerland.
	Dürrenmatt Center, Neuchâtel, Switzerland.
	Jean Tinguely Museum, Basel, Switzerland.
	Commercial and residential building, Merate, Italy.
1993	Highway noise protection wall, Chiasso, Switzerland.
	Kyobo Office Tower, Seoul, South Corea.
	Reconstruction of a town building in Mendrisio, Switzerland.
	Set design Medea, Opernhaus, Zurich, Switzerland.
	Scientific College, Città della Pieve, Italy.
	Service station City Quinto, Piotta, Switzerland.
	Parish Church in Seriate, Bergamo, Italy.
	Exhibition Friedrich Dürrenmatt, Kunsthaus, Zurich, Switzerland.
1994	Armchair Charlotte.
	Restructure of the Querini Stampalia Foundation, Venice, Italy.
1995	Public Library, Bergamo, Italy.
	Family house in Muzzano, Switzerland.
	Set design for "Ippolito", Stadttheater Basel, Switzerland.
	Noah's Ark Sculpture Garden, Jerusalem, Israel.
	Clock Blumenzeit for Mondaine Watch.
	Refurbishment of the lobby Kyobo Building, Seoul, South Corea.
	Restoration Museum Vincenzo Vela, Ligornetto, Switzerland.
	Municipal Library, Dortmund, Germany.
	Entrance gate to the Tarot Garden of Niki de Saint Phalle, Garavicchio, Italy.

1996	Building renovation Republic National Bank, Lugano, Switzerland.
	Benkert industrial building, Altershausen, Germany.
	Cymbalista Synagogue and Jewish Heritage Center, Tel Aviv, Israel.
	Monument Summit of the Americas, Santa Cruz de la Sierra, Bolivia.
	Museum of Modern Art of Rovereto and Trento, Rovereto, Italy.
	Pavilion for the exhibition Kolonihaven, Kopenhagen, Denmark.
	Ceiling lamp Mendrisio; in collaboration with Dante Solcà.
	Tata Consultancy Office Building, Noida, New Delhi, India.
	Monument to Jean Marc Reiser, Montparnasse Cemetery, Paris, France.
1997	Watch Botta for Pierre Junod.
	New funicular stations in Orselina and Cardada, Locarno, Switzerland.
	Wall tapestry in the Abbey of Moutier d'Ahun, France.
	National Bank of Greece, Athens, Greece.
	Extension of the Bodmer Library, Cologny, Geneva, Switzerland.
1998	Glacier 3000, Les Diablerets, Switzerland.
	Family house in Königsberg, Germany.
	Exhibition Nag Arnoldi, Lugano, Switzerland.
	Tower in Moron, Switzerland.
	Watch Sfmoma for Mondaine Watch.
	Remake of the church façade in Genestrerio, Ticino, Switzerland.
1999	Wood model of Borromini's church San Carlo alle Quattro Fontane, Lugano, Switzerland.
	Pitchers Mia and Tua for Alessi.
	Wine Cellars Petra, Suvereto, Italy.
	Harting Offices, Minden, Germany.
	Tata Offices Center, Hyderabad, India.
	Urban furniture Pausa for Benkert.
	Cultural center in Leuk, Switzerland.
2000	Wine and water glass for Cleto Munari.
	Weekend houses in Cardada, Switzerland.
	Central bus terminal in Lugano, Switzerland.
	National Insurance Company of Greece, Athens, Greece.
	Art Museum Bechtler, Charlotte, North Carolina, USA.
2001	Residences in Haarlemmermeer, The Netherlands.
	Office building in Vimodrone, Milan, Italy.
	Parish church in Attendorn, Germany.
	Church Santo Volto, Turin, Italy.
	Requalification of the ancient port area, Trieste, Italy.
	Art Museum, Tsinghma University, Beijing, China.
	Kindergarden in Rosà, Italy.
	Privat chapel in Azzano di Seravezza, Italy.
	Tower for the Pinocchio's Friends Park, Carlo Collodi National Foundation, Collodi, Italy.
	De Monarch Office Buildings, Den Hague, The Netherlands.
	Restoration and reconstruction of the Scala Theater, Milan, Italy.
2002	Glass bottle for Valser mineral water, Italy.
	Hotel and reception facilities in Pietrelcina, Italy.

Credits

San Francisco Museum of Modern Art
Project: 1989–1992
Client: San Francisco Museum of Modern Art Foundation
Architect of record: Hellmuth, Obata & Kassabaum, Inc., San Francisco, CA

Chapel of Saint Mary of the Angels
Project: 1990–1992
Client: Egidio Cattaneo

Church of Saint John the Baptist
Project 1986/1992
Client: Mogno Church Reconstruction Association
Architect of record: Giovanluigi Dazio, Locarno

The Cymbalista Synagogue and Jewish Heritage Center
Project: 1996
Client: Paulette and Norbert Cymbalista

Municipal Library
Project: 1995
Client: City of Dortmund represented by the Odeum Grundstücksverwaltungs-gesellschaft mbH&Co.
Architect of record: Gert Vette, Köln
Structural engineer: Klemens Pelle, Dortmund

Villa Redaelli
Project: 1996
Client: Leader srl, Milano
Architect of record: Anna Bruna Vertemati, Fabiano Redaelli, Vimercate

Dürrenmatt Center
Project: 1992–1997
Client: Federal Financial Departement, Federal Departement for Construction and Logistics
User: Swiss archives of literature, National Swiss Library
Architect of record: Urscheler & Arrigo SA, Neuchâtel

National Sports Center
Project : 1990/1993
Client: Federal Financial Department, Federal Department for Construction and Logistics
User: Federal Fepartment for Sports

Noah's Ark Sculpture garden with Niki de Saint Phalle
Project: 1995
Client: The Jerusalem Foundation, City of Jerusalem
Architect of record: Henry Raviv, Miller & Blum, Haifa

National Bank of Greece
with Morfo Papanikolaou, Irena Sakellaridou, Maria Pollani ass.architects, Thessaloniki
Project: 1996/1999
Client: National Bank of Greece, Athens
Civil engineer: Vasis Sysm/Ch. Mylonas and P. Antoniadou
Special Consultancies: Dr. K. Demiri (architect), Th.Timagenis (acoustic studies),
Dr. K. Tsakalides (civil engineering), K. Theologidou (conservation architect), N. Zographos
(interior design)

Harting Offices
Project: 1999
Client: Harting Deutschland GmBh&Co. KG - Margrit and Dietmar Harting
Architect of record: Planungsgruppe Minden

Museum of Modern Art of Rovereto and Trento with Ing. Giulio Andreolli, Rovereto
Project: 1988/93
Client: City of Rovereto and autonomous province of Trento